Full Count

THE BOOK OF METS POETRY

Frank Messina

The Lyons Press
Guilford, Connecticut
An imprint of The Globe Pequot Press

The Lyons Press is an imprint of The Globe Pequot Press.

Project manager: David Legere
Interior designer: Sheryl P. Kober
Layout artist: Kim Burdick

Library of Congress Cataloging-in-Publication Data
is available on file.

ISBN 978-1-59921-557-0

Printed in the United States of America

10 9 8 7 6 5 4 3 2 1

Dedicated to my father,
who taught me how to confront victory, failure,
screwballs, change-ups and full counts.

Contents

Part IV: Working the Count

Part V: Up and In

Part VI: Foul Ball

Part VII: In the Stands

Part VIII: Again, The Signs

Part IX: Full Count

Acknowledgments

The author wishes to thank Ron Whitehead for his generous editorial support and advice. Special thanks to John Messina for proofreading and Tony Broy for conceptual considerations; David Amram for his kind creative and business suggestions; Mark Reese, Brad Kahn and Charlie Samuels; Max Siegal and the entire staff at Mets Weekly, Tupelo-Honey Productions and SNY-TV. Steve Somers and Joe Benigno and WFAN. Thanks to my loving family and loyal friends. I am and shall forever be indebted. And to the fans, both known and unknown. See you at the game!

Author's Preface

A young journalist once asked me if the game of baseball is a metaphor for real life. After crumpling my beer can and nearly tossing the smartass out of the bar, I paused and reflected.

I thought of that famous photograph of Babe Ruth, his back to the camera, the number three, his frail body, shoulders slightly hunched, hat off in humility to the throngs of fans before him. I also thought about the famous photograph of the sailor kissing the gal in Times Square, the raising of the flag at Iwo Jima, and again by three firefighters on 9/11.

A good poem is a "snapshot," a moment caught by using words to create an image for the reader.

I decided to compile the more than one-hundred pieces for this book with the purpose of sharing "snapshots" from a life as a baseball fan, a Mets fan.

However, through the process, the book evolved into a twisted auto-biography. A story of a life of continuous curve balls, incredible luck, amazing victory, and sudden loss. A life where the game once served as an escape, but soon became an obsession. A place where baseball isn't a metaphor for real life, but IS real life. A life always on the verge, at the edge, and endlessly remains a "full count."

Frank Messina
2/2/09, Jersey City, NJ

Part I
Stepping to the Plate

It was I, Mrs. Wiley

It was I, Mrs. Wiley
who swiped
your garbage pail lids
and turned them into first, second and third,
It was I who lifted
the welcome mat from your front stoop
-unbeknownst to you-
It was I who proudly placed it down
and crowned it "pitcher's mound"

It was I, Mrs. Wiley
who laughed out loud
as balls ricocheted
off the side of your house
and into your pruned rosebushes
and it was I, Mrs. Wiley who
cracked a home-run
through your second-story window
It was I, Mrs. Wiley
who hid behind the Apple tree
as you hollered through the broken panes

It was I, Mrs. Wiley
who had the chance to confess
when I saw you in Church
but instead, looked away
and it was I, Mrs. Wiley
who your dog chased
through the pickets
without looking both ways

and it was I who watched
you repair the window
with putty and tape,
stifling my giggles
as you balanced the ladder
It was I, Mrs. Wiley,
who broke your window
and caused you such despair
yes, Mrs. Wiley, it was I

Barker

When I grow up,
I want to be a Ballpark Barker
and bark at the ballpark people,
"Scorecards, Yearbooks!"
I'll bellow from the belly of my being,
"Hot dogs, get your hot dogs!"
I'll sing sweet songs of
"Ice Cream! Peanuts! Cracker Jack!"
I'll boast from the barrel of my body,
"Beer here, yo-Beer, get yer cold beer!"

When I grow up,
I want to be a Ballpark Barker
and bark at the ballpark people,
"Pennants! T-shirts! Souvenirs!"
I'll send soft and salty treats
through the ballpark's crowded seats
"Hot pretzels, Hot pretzels!"
"French fries!" and "Wings!"
Rain delay? What rain delay?
only smiles sprinkle with the sound
of "Ice cold lemonade!"

When I grow up,
I want to be a Ballpark Barker
and bark at the ballpark people,
"Cotton Candy! Cotton Candy!"
through the curvy concourse I'll cry,
"Kettle Korn! Kettle Korn!"
through the hallways I'll heave,

"Hamburgers! Hamburgers!
ketchup, mayo, onions and cheese!"

When I grow up,
I want to be a Ballpark Barker
and bark at the ballpark people,
"I am the ballpark barker!"
listen to me bark at the ballpark people
buying, buying, buying, from the
Ballpark Barker

Spring Training

Sun shines on diamond
two birds on a citrus limb
ball meets bat, a crack!

Mrs. Brickman

First memory,
Kindergarten, Mrs. Brickman,
show-and-tell, Tommie Agee baseball card

Holding it up, like a medallion
kids smiling, Agee smiling,
my moment in the spotlight

Later caught chewing gum,
Mrs. Brickman grabs collar,
shoves me into corner

Facing wall, alone, trembling
hands in pockets, searching for Tommie Agee,
my friend in the baseball card

Mrs. Brickman grabs collar, twists,
"Is this what you're looking for?"
holds up the card, a medallion

She rips it in half, again and again,
then throws the pieces at me

First memory, kindergarten

Tears and Tommie Agee

Mrs. Brickman

The Blue Glove

T.J. and I never had much in common,
except that we were both abused by the same teachers,
but all those back-room punishments we endured
couldn't steal our dream of playing ball under the sun

T.J. had a pigskin glove, tanned with shoe polish
his grandfather gave him straight from the shine-box,
I had one I found abandoned in an old gym bag,
blue glove. As soon as I laid my eyes on it,
it spoke to me, different, misfit, comfortable

Thirty years later, I bump into Pedro Martinez,
ask why he uses a blue glove, Pedro smiles and says,
"I've always used a blue glove, different, comfortable."

Smiling Child

A mitt hangs on hook
dust, cobwebs, a creaking door;
small hand reaches up

Detention with Mr. Pigari

Gazing out window, daydreaming
Mets patch in my hands,
"Did you hear what I said, Messina?"

Another detention

Mop floor, empty garbage
wipe blackboard with sponge,
"Butchie, Joe, come smack Messina around!"

Hanging from door hook, I take the jabs,
down-jacket rips, explodes, feathers everywhere
I fall, then stand, Mets patch still in hands

Dad Takes Me to School

8 a.m. dad takes my hand
going to see the principal

what did I do now?

you've done nothing son

dad and principal in the office

principal emerges white as a ghost

teachers never touched me again

"Playing" for The Mets

I grew up in a Yankee town. A small town, but a Yankee town. Long before baseball players lived in mansions, they lived in smaller things called "homes".
Not far from my family's home, down Blanche Avenue, across the railroad tracks, past John's Pizzeria, not far from where I first kissed the tough, but cute red-headed Roxanne, lived Catfish Hunter. Across from Hunter lived Gene Michael. A Yankee. In fact, Norwood was the home to several Yankee players; Thurmon Munson, Ron Guidry, Don Gullet to name a few. Every shop in town had pictures of the Yankees. You couldn't get away from it. In short, it was Mets fan hell.

However, this was August, 1978, and if I remember correctly, it was a hot, humid, sticky summer day. Andy Widholm and I were bored as two sugar-induced ten year-old demons could be. Andy was a schoolteacher's worst nightmare, and when we got together, we were a regular *Butch Cassidy and the Sundance Kid,* high on sucrose, glucose, concentrated corn syrup and red food dye #3. Of course, this was long before parents succumbed to medicating their kids with mind-altering drugs when in fact they could have just as easily refrained from pouring that gallon of RC Cola down our throats.

As Andy and I sat on the curb munching our Pop Rocks and counting how many spider eggs we found in our Bubble Yum, a blue Chevy Nova rumbled down Carter Street; Catfish Hunter. The car pulled up the driveway next door to Andy's home. Catfish got out with another buddy of his, Graig Nettles. Yankees. They were just coming back from a day game against the Kansas City Royals.

Seeing them was nothing special, since Catfish lived next door to Andy. But, somehow I knew this day would be different. And different it was. Catfish picked up a wiffle-ball from his front porch and threw it over to Andy. "Here's your ball, kid," he said. Andy looked over at me through his devilish, dirty-blond hair and menacing grin and said, "Let's go!" I grabbed the bat leaning against his mom's Delta 88 and we darted for the street.

As Andy and I played ball in the street, Nettles and Hunter cracked beers in the driveway. After a couple of tosses, Andy yelled over, "Hey Catfish, what are you looking at? You're pitching. Nettles, you're playing outfield. This is the World Series. Game seven, bottom of the ninth, tie game 3-3 at Shea. Me and Frankie are the Mets and we're gonna kick your Yankee butts in!"

Catfish and Nettles took to the street. Andy was up first. He was a feisty kid. One who didn't like being placated either. "Pitch me something real, Catfish," he yelled. Nettles, beer in one hand, shouted from his spot as the designated outfielder for our impromptu World Series game on Carter Street, "Up and in, Fish. Don't let the kid make me run."

After settling in, Andy cracked a 2-1 change-up over Nettles head, past Mr. Rainie's Pinto and deep into Mrs. Lutzo's tomato plants. By the time Nettles dug through the vines and relayed the throw back to Catfish Hunter, Andy had made it safely to third base. Andy was beaming, Mrs. Lutzo was screaming and I was up next.

"C'mon Frankie, you could do it," hollered Andy. My hands began to sweat. Catfish pitched a fastball just outside the home plate manhole cover. I could tell it wasn't going to be a dead give-away. Andy and I were going to have to earn this win or lose everything. In short, this was *the real thing*. The count was one ball, one squished tomato under Nettle's foot and one cute redhead peering from the outfield bleacher-box windows of our "Carter Street Stadium".

"This is it," I thought. "I'm gonna do it." As I pushed the strands of hair from my face, Nettles moved closer to the third base bag, hoping to get a tag on Andy should I pop the ball up. Full count, bottom of the ninth inning, game seven of the World Series, the go-ahead run at third base and it's all up to me and my filthy, pop-rock, sugar-glazed hands and "Grand Way special" sneakered feet.

I took a deep breath and settled in, focusing only on hitting the ball. Andy's hollering faded into the back-ground. For a moment, it was just me and Catfish. And I was going to do it for my team, the Mets.

Hunter served a belt-high fast ball over the plate and I swung. All I remember is Andy jumping for joy as the ball lined past a diving Graig Nettles allowing Andy to score the winning run. We had won the World Series! Andy and I hugged each other, jumping up and down, hollering so loud the neighbors came out to see what in hell was going on. Andy pumped his fists high in the air as we did imitation mock laughs of Vinnie Barbarino and Arnold Horshack.

Nettles and Catfish picked up their beers, smiled, then one of them said, "Kids, go home and eat now. Good game. You deserve it."

Later that evening, walking home, heading down Carter Street, around Broadway, cutting through the railroad tracks, I heard a familiar voice coming from the friendly, yellow-lit porch door of Roxanne's house. "Hey Frankie," she said, running over to me. "Congratulations. You won!" Then, she planted a kiss on my cheek. Before I could even blush, she ran back inside. The door closed and I continued on my way; the hero, the slugger, the dreamer, the newly indoctrinated die-hard baseball fanatic. Just a kid, but one who just tasted the quiet glory of being a Mets fan.

Part II
Getting the Signs

The Art of Restraint and Cool Excuses

She was intrigued
or perhaps just drunk
but she mustered enough courage
to ask me out to lunch, a show, music
I appreciated her opinions and admired the way
she carried herself,
so I popped the big question on her:
"Mets-Braves, gorgeous summer night, you know?"

"Not tonight," she said

"But, you can come upstairs with me," she said
with a Mona Lisa smile

Part of me wanted to go up there with her

I thought for a moment, then said,
"No, not tonight, I'm headed to the game,
Mets-Braves, gorgeous summer night, you know?"

She gently shook her head, turned,
then disappeared into the apartment building

Later, when I got to the stadium
I studied the empty seat beside me,
placed a napkin in the center, then my beer,
Then I shifted my eyes toward the part of me
that wanted to go upstairs with her
and said, "Not tonight, pal. Not tonight."

Wild Elephants

There's a herd
of wild elephants in my home
not sure how they arrived
first I called some friends,
served Sangria, chips and salsa
sliced fruit, cheese and wine
but
soon enough a wild holler broke out,
my friends grew tusks, trunks and tails
and proceeded to trample, then stampeded
hurling trees in their wake,
rocking, standing on hind legs then
crashing down on all fours

There's a herd
of wild elephants in my home
not sure how they arrived
my friends I called, but they turned
to wretched, horrid pachyderms
stomped and caused a mess
but
I've learned from their beastly ways
and cease to call them guests,
now I watch the game alone
and pull the plug from my phone,
just in case my thick-skinned friends
get the nerve to call again

Magic Hands

At the benefit show, D meets David Wright
shakes his hand, sneaks a hug

I bet he hits a home-run tomorrow!

That's right sweets, you got magic hands

Next day, D and I watch game

David hits a home-run

little girl smiles, claps magic hands

Dust of the Departed Ones

Long after the final pitch is thrown
and the stadium lights resigned,
Long after the players have gone
the grounds crew raked and limed

The night people come, scale walls
envelopes, urns, baskets in hand
Fulfilling wishes of dear departed ones
by spreading their ashes on the land

Dust of the departed now one with the game
soaked in soil, whence they came
to rise and cheer, family and guests
spirits and ghosts sing, "Let's got Mets!"

Caught in the gust of a pitcher's arm,
kicked in the cloud of a runner's slide,
pressed to cleats, caps and uniforms
the dust it scatters and intertwines

The night people smile from the stands
filled with joy, they clap their hands,
knowing they served their loved ones true
by spreading ashes, as night people do

Soon after the game begins
listen closely for words on the wind,
the departed who sing that song by name,
"Take Me Out to the Ball Game"

A Simple Thank You

At the game,
soldier, wife and little girl,
I stop and thank the man
for his service to the country,
he extends his hand and firmly shakes
and I continue through the stands

What is Losing?

Losing is an elevator car
pulled down by the gravity of failure

f
a
l
l
i
n
g

from throat, gut
chest cavity, to the
innards of your being

Losing is a hundred "what-ifs" and "if-onlys"
being replayed in your mind,
replayed in your mind,
if only...
if only...

"if only" never comes up
until you lose again

-if only, what if, if only, what if-

Losing is "game over", elevator cars falling,
house of cards tumbling, a million "what-ifs"
refusing to dislodge from throat, chest, gut
-if only, what if, if only, what if-

Losing wouldn't be so bad
if only you could turn back the hands of time,
undo what's been done, but you cannot undo time
you can only keep replaying it in your mind

-if only, what if, if only, what if-

Part III
Settling In

Rainbow Over Shea

Rain sweeps through,
but sweeps not the smiles
from Shea

not on this day!

Storm clouds roll,
but roll not the promise
from Shea

not on this day!

Winds blow,
but blow not the hope
from Shea

not on this day!

Sun breaks through, a rainbow,
Mets take the field

on this day!

House of Horrors

I went to the House of Horrors
brought battle gear, Mets cap and jersey
expecting torment and ill-will toward my team,
instead, the Braves crowd treated us with
dignity, respect, gracious southern charm,
and better yet, we swept them
with the help of Pedro's arm

Why Solving World Peace is Impossible

I hereby challenge
all world leaders to immediately
lay down your arms,
open your minds
and assemble
in a fair game of baseball

You will be given
twenty-seven outs over nine innings
to prove your worthiness, fortitude,
resilience, strategic prowess
and sportsmanship to the world

If you achieve victory,
you shall be celebrated by the masses

If you fail, you must accept the loss
with dignity and honor,
there shall be no shame in defeat
as there shall be no dishonor inflicted
by the hands of the victor
now and forever,
is this understood?

Injured by What I Can No Longer Do

I awoke with joint pain
like never before,
back aching from years of repeated motion,
elbow enflamed, sensation of small razors under skin
but
I'm in the stands watching young bucks
push bodies around like machines,
hyper-extending knees, stretching hammies
like rubber bands, which pains me to even see,
maybe that's why I'm in pain:
from watching human male forms do
what I can no longer do

How dare them!

Jesse Orosco

Weary, mound he kneels
sweat, blood to soil in drops
Autumn joy explodes

The Leaping Gazelle

There's a "leaping gazelle"
on the New York Mets
And his name is Endy Chavez

He chases fly balls
from right to left
flying, diving, robbing

defying the laws of physics

There he is!
Sliding, lunging, recovering
doubling-up runners in scoring position
(left there only wishing
they had a chance against
the graceful Metropolitan)

Yes, there's a "leaping gazelle"
on the New York Mets
and his name is Endy Chavez

At the plate
the "leaping gazelle" turns into a jaguar,
a cheetah, a gritty lion on the prowl
(Fastball hit-on and pierced up the middle
finding its way thru the hole!)
jets ignite from under his feet
sliding safely into second, third and home
the crowd rises and cheers
Endy comes up smiling,

uniform a dusty mess
and
the look of victory in his eyes

He can fool 50,000 fans
and an ace on the mound
with a surprise drag-bunt
that makes the crowd stand on end
the team celebrates . . . once again
'cause Endy has saved the day

Yes, there's a "leaping gazelle"
on the New York Mets
and his name is Endy Chavez

The player with pure, New-York-Mets-hustle
off the fence, against the fence
at the plate
always in the clutch
always in a rally
always full of surprises
always Endy, Endy, Endy
and a happy ending to all!

Yes, there's a "leaping gazelle"
on the New York Mets
and his name is Endy Chavez
and
his name
is
Endy Chavez!

Subway Series 2000

The city has waited three generations
and now it's come true: Mets and Yanks
under October's blue moon

New York is shining like Emerald City
Empire State glows orange and blue
held firmly in a base of white-lighted hue

The people in the streets are singing
"Piazza, Leiter, Jeter, Clemens"
the fans are in baseball's seventh heaven

The game is today, the hour is now
The love of our teams, the love of our city
manifested, realized in this "subway series"

Mets against defending World Champs
Yanks against the Wild Card Mets
what turmoil, what joy the city awaits!
the heart of the city pulses and beats!

Chills run up and down the spine
of the gorgeous, New York City skyline
Brooklyn, Queens, The Bronx, Staten Island
New York-New York in the year 2000!

Just a Game

In 1986, Bob Millikan and I went to a dozen games together. My parents had amazed the entire family on Christmas Day, 1985, by purchasing two seats for the upcoming 1986 season; a gift for the family. But, there was a catch. Since I was the youngest, I had to wait for my older brothers to cancel out before I could nail a seat to the game.

Bob and I would cruise over the George Washington Bridge in his '62 convertible to catch the Mets at Shea. School nights were no exception. It was an easy decision, algebra or Mets games? We watched Doc Gooden outlast Nolan Ryan, watched Strawberry homer over the right field wall, caught a foul ball off Carter's bat, and paid a grungy older fellow to buy us beers at the concession stand, flirted with the girls in the row behind us who claimed they were "Keith's chicks." And dreamed of the inevitable October.

In early September, Bob went off to college at Stockton State. I promised him we'd go to the World Series together but warned he may have to cut a class or two to make it. He agreed, and we parted ways for what turned out to be an eternity.

In the early morning hours of September 11, 1986, Bob flipped his '62 convertible on Highway 9 in Somers Point, New Jersey. An early Thursday morning and eighteen years of innocence had vanished forever. My heart was broken. Somehow, I had to get through this tragedy, but how?

The next game I saw was on September 17 at Shea Stadium. Sadness was in my heart, but my older brother

Robert urged me to come along with him and his lovely gal, Sue. Not only that, we managed to get four of my pals into the game. Robert carried on his shoulder a giant tube filled with punch-hole confetti. "It's gonna happen tonight" he said. "The Mets will clinch the NL East."

By the eighth inning, our third-base-line seats were getting overcrowded with thousands of pressing fans. Something magical was about to happen, something scary, something I will never forget, but something magical. When the final out was recorded, fifty thousand orange-and-blue-clad maniacs carried us crazy 18-year-olds onto the field. A human gush of madness and glory. . .and the rest is history.

For a moment, I forgot about the sadness that wallowed in the caverns of my heart; the sadness and torture of losing a friend so tragically. For a moment, I was innocent again. And baseball had everything to do with it.

On October 25, 1986, I was at the legendary "Game Six" standing in the upper decks with my other older brother John by my side. Back then, the Mets gave season ticket holders an option to purchase more post-season tickets. So, my mother and father were down below enjoying the third-base-line view while John and I were upstairs. But, it didn't matter where our seats were located. We were at "the game".

In the bottom of the tenth inning with two outs, all of my hopes had faded. Only a few weeks ago, I promised Bob we'd go to the World Series together. He was gone. The Mets were losing and everything I had hoped for this season was coming to a close. More broken dreams and more sadness. I apologized to Bob in silent prayer for not coming through for him. Somehow I had equated this game with the happenstance of my life. If the Mets failed, I failed. It was that simple.

I sat down and tried to shake off the misery. To add insult to injury, a few Red Sox fans took pictures of us gloomy, broken-hearted Mets fans. I still remember two red-faced, red-dressed, red-haired Red Sox fans shouting to us, "You lose, go bock to your caw!" At that point, I couldn't take it. I stood up and yelled out from the upper decks, my voice drowned out by throngs of fans, airplanes flying overhead and cracker jack vendors. "Do it for Bob! Do it for Bob!"

The rest was a complete blur as pandemonium broke lose at Shea Stadium. When Mookie Wilson hit that slow roller up the first baseline through Buckner's legs, all of our hopes and dreams had become real again. "Ray Knight around third, the Mets win. The Mets win." For a moment, I was innocent again. And baseball had everything to do with it.

Two days later, Game Seven morning, my father came into my room and asked if I enjoyed seeing game six. I realized there were only four seats and I was sure he and Mom were going to the game, and probably John and Robert, too. Afterall, I was the runt and I had my fill this time around. I did not expect to go see the final game of the World Series.

"You know Frankie" he said. "You saw an amazing game the other night. When I was younger than you, I would listen to the New York Giants on the radio. I would be rooting for Willie Mays. Living in the Bronx, I was a minority Giants fan," he said. "We were hard to come by. Anyhow, as you know, John and Robert will be going to the game."

"Yeah, Dad I know," I replied. "Of course, Mom is going, because she's Mom," he quipped. "Yeah, Dad I know," I shrugged.

Then, his eyes turned to mine and he said, "Son, do you want to see history be made?" "Yeah, Dad, of course," I said. "Well, Frankie, go see history be made. Have a great time tonight, kid. Here's your ticket."

That's what kind of man my father was; a generous, amazing, romantic who understood how a simple gesture could lift a kid's spirit, searing a memory in his mind that would last a lifetime. And baseball had everything to do with it.

Part IV
Working the Count

Turk Wendell

I'd like to go bowhunting with Turk Wendell
gut a moose and mount it in my living room,
but Turk's not a man who likes company, so I'm told
-Turk with a necklace of fangs, out on the wild plains-
no lines to hop, no crouching-standing catchers,
Just Turk in the jungle, collecting claws and teeth

I'd like to go shark fishing with Turk Wendell
chum the waters, drop the line and gaff a leaping beast,
but Turk's not a man who likes company, so I'm told
-Turk with a toothbrush, chasing Jaws around the deep-
no umpire rolling ball, no crosses on the mound
Just Turk and his tackle, on the high and rolling sea

I'd like to track a polar bear with Turk Wendell
snowshoe our way across the frozen tundra,
but Turk's not a man who likes company, so I'm told
-Turk with a bucket of ninety-nine knives-
no dugouts, just igloos, no rosin bags to pound,
Just Turk on the tundra, hunting 999 pounds

I'd like to go deer hunting with Turk Wendell
leather gloves, loaded guns and drop a twelve-point buck,
but Turk's not a man who likes company, so I'm told
-Turk with just one glove, the other he tossed around-
no waving, brushing, pounding between each pitch
Just Turk in the forest, where the wild things live

Keith Hernandez

Look at Keith in the booth!
tossing Tootsie Pops to the youth

I remember Keith on first
diving, sliding, reaching, grabbing
hitting clutch, rounding third

Look at Keith in the booth!
tossing Tootsie Pops to the youth

I remember Keith in '83, four, five and six
the fans we cheered, "Let's Got Mex!"
He tipped his cap, we waved and Keith waved back
fans roared with a crack of the bat

Look at Keith in the booth!
tossing Tootsie Pops to the youth

How do I know he throws them down?
I am one of those ageless clowns

Look at Keith in the booth!
tossing Tootsie Pops to the youth

José Reyes

Jose` Reyes is by far
the most exciting
player to watch in baseball

why?

because Jose`, Jose`, Jose`
has jets in his legs

See him run, see him go
Jose`, Jose`, Jose`
stole another base today!

Jose` Reyes is a
pitcher's worst nightmare,
when on base, watch him there!

Leading halfway down the line
bouncing, prancing, eyes aglow and wide
Pick him off? Not a chance,
to the bag he slides

See him run, see him go
Jose`, Jose`, Jose`
stole another base today!

On third base
he never ceases to amaze,
taunting pitchers from the bag,
sending them to rage

Pitcher fails to pause
the ump he yells, "now you've balked!"
and Jose` skips happily home

Jose`, Jose`, Jose`
stole another base today!

Don the Red Sox Fan

Don lives upstairs
but today he's in the garden
with Samuel Adams and Khaki Jeans;
eyes pinned to the pages
of a James Burke mystery novel,
He's worked a long day
and even a Boston transplant
deserves peace and quiet once in a while

but it's 7 p.m.

and I'm pacing around, checking stats,
injury reports, analyzing every word of the pre-game
wondering what's up with our pitching staff
and someone please tell me
where is El Duque?
but
there's Don, feet propped up,
plate of fresh fruit, Rib eye slow-cooking on the grill
and all I can find
is some leftover Chinese food,
broken bits of Xanax, maybe a Zoloft or two
fumbling through take-out menus,
medical prescriptions and scorecards
getting ready for the game
and then
I look back out the window
at Don in the garden,
wondering how a self-proclaimed, die-hard Sox fan
can be so calm and collected

so I check the schedule
and notice the Sox are playing the Yankees
no wonder he's not worried
and
four hours later
his team has already won
but my team is tied at three in the twelfth!
storm clouds rolling in, winds kicking up
here comes the tarp

and it's 12 a.m.

My head is starting to hurt,
nails bitten off their nubs
empty Chinese food containers, prescription bottles
and there's Don in the garden
full-bellied, fast asleep, moon shining upon his face
and just when I'd been tortured enough
a kid in his first major league at-bat
comes up with the go-ahead run at third
and plucks one into center field for
the game winning single
and I holler so loud
I wake Don in the garden
who collects his barbecue gear, empty bottles
and clangs his way down the hallway

I open the door and say, "Mets won!"
and there's Don, ruddy-faced
rubbing eyes, checking a text message
and says, "ah look Sox won too, goodnight Frank"
makes his way up the stairs

while I shut the door, turn out the lights
and lay my weary bones down on the couch
to get some rest
because tomorrow is another day
yes, another day at the opera,
another day on the high anxiety,
Mets roller-coaster ride of suicidal delirium

Ageless

Old man opens gift
two tickets to the ballgame,
a gray-haired child smiles

Baseball Study

Round, leather white ball,
five ounces, nine-inch diameter,
wrapped in two segments of
conditioned leather, separated by
one-hundred and eight red,
waxed, cotton thread stitches,
stamped blue lettering, Rawlings logo
stamped above anterior stitching,
"Official Major League Baseball,
Allan H. Selig, Commissioner" stamped
between anterior and posterior stitching,
Major League Baseball logo stamped
below anterior stitching,
earthy bouquet, mild, salty flavor

Where I am From

I am from a place
where the sun rises and shines,
glitters off buildings,
a city of steel cathedrals,

I am from a place called "America!"

I am from a place
where spring begins on Opening Day
and winter, the World Series
I am from a place where barriers
were broken, dreams realized and justice prevailed,

I am from a place called "America!"

I am from an imperfect place,
where struggle, strife and prejudice
wreaked havoc on our name
but climbed up from our broken past
sent Jackie Robinson to the game

I am from a place called "America!"

I am from a place, the flag we raise
is a symbol of the people,
white, black, yellow, red and tan
together rise up and sing, "We're Americans!"

I am from a place where we strive to live
by a Constitution and the rules,
but at times make errors, and the game we lose

I am from a place called "America!"

I am from a place where freedom reigns
on the open field, under the lights
under the flag of stars and stripes

I am from a place called "America!"

Fifty-Thousand Different Ways

Everyone has a way to get to Shea

N, Q, R, #7 Willets Point,
PATH, Penn, Long Island Rail Road,
Port Washington line
GWB, Cross Bronx,
Tri-Borough, Grand Central, exit nine

Directions, directions, directions
fifty-thousand different ways,
north, south, east or west,
We all end up at Shea!

Northern Blvd, exit 9E,
Northern Blvd, exit 9W,
P1, P9, or P2

Everyone has a way to get to Shea

Van Wyck/Whitestone
Linden Blvd exit 14,
College Point Boulevard, Roosevelt Ave.

Directions, directions, directions
fifty-thousand different ways
north, south, east or west,
We all end up at Shea!

Everyone has a way to get to Shea

Van Wyck, Northern Blvd Exit 13W
Long Island Expressway,
Midtown Tunnel,
Grand Central-west, exit 22A
College Point Boulevard

Directions, directions, directions
fifty-thousand different ways
north, south, east or west,
We all end up at Shea!

Take a bus, Q44 or the Q66
Ferry, a civilized way,
From Highlands, NJ,
the Seastreak
New York Fast Ferry too

Directions, directions, directions
fifty-thousand different ways
north, south, east or west,
We all end up at Shea!

Spring Training Poem

I awake,
peanut butter and jelly, whole wheat
vitamins, banana
soy milk
fifty push-ups
fifty sit-ups,
one-hundred, sixty-two games
one-hundred, sixty-two poems

Eight Lines for Injury

He staggers to position,
kneecap pried, crowbar

He limps to first base bag,
ankle rolled, sprained

He shudders from batter's box,
up and in, bell rung

He collects, breathes, stands
returns and settles in

Double Play, Side Retired

Three ducks on the pond
Kaz Matsui to the plate
fifty-thousand "boos"

More Fun with Kaz

Kaz in batter's box
white ball flies three times past plate
fifty-thousand "boos"

Part V
Up and In

Striking Father Out, One Summer Day

He grabbed the handle of the bat
grinned proudly and stepped to the plate

seemed like yesterday when he
taught me how to swing

now he's in the box
balance giving in to Parkinson's

I pitch the ball with some heat
strike one, he said, pitch it again

You alright? sure I'm fine, pitch the ball
I throw one slowly, strike two

I search for an excuse not to throw next pitch:
barbecue's ready, food's on the table

I looked down at the mound, same browned hump
where he taught me how to settle in and focus

Pitch the ball, he said, don't be afraid
I did and strike three came

Father walked to patio,
Mom asked how was the game

Father grinned and said,
your son can't pitch worth a damn!

Victory's Door

Do you know what it's like
to be chased by the Ghost of Failure
while staring through Victory's door?

Of course you do, you're a Mets fan!

Juiced

I saw you grow, fall, fail
as no man should grow, fall, fail
plant yourself to mound, box, field
hurl, hit, climb like no man
should hurl, hit, climb

I saw athletic forms morph
into hulking behemoths,
as no other form shall morph,
forehead protruding into
nine-inning horrors

I saw school kids idolizing,
fantasizing, needling themselves
toward the big league dream,
murdered in a criminal, cardiac
attempt to reach major league

I saw a system that turned
head, heart, eyes,
fooled into eight-figure contracts,
record books, but no Hall of Fame

I saw an entire generation
duped by poisoned achievements,
imprisoned by the desire to win

and failure to understand the price to be paid
for the incessant desire to manipulate the game,
but
you cannot manipulate the game,
only degrade, destroy and undermine
and that's exactly what you've done

We Know! (2006)

For twenty years all we heard was, "Ya Gotta Believe!"

and since '86, It was "You Gotta Bereave!"

How many times have we been so close, yet so far?

But, this is 2006, and for once, we know
Yes, we believed, but now we know

When Carlos Beltran
closes games with walk-off homers,
We know it when
José, José, José, rounds bases
quicker than a magician
Yes, you heard it here,
I've now coined him,
The Dominican Magician

We know!

We believed in '73
We believed in 2000
but, now we understand
something different is going on
at Shea; a chemistry beyond doubt
that we are going all the way
How, you may ask? Because

We Know

No longer do we worry about
being three runs down heading into the eighth
not with my man Paul Lo Duca,
The Beltran and Delgado due up
we know David is gonna get it right
we're gonna win this time around
not because we believe, but because

We know!

The baseball gods are with us
and the planets are aligned
Pedro, Glavine, El Duque are just fine
Aaron Heilman our bridge to the ninth·
Billy Wagner adds just enough drama
but when the game is over
the opponent feels the trauma
We're gonna win, win, win
we're gonna do it this time
not because we believe
but
because we know!
do we know?
Yes,

We know!

One Hundred and One

Elevator door opens
pediatric cancer ward,
one hundred courageous kids

Elevator door opens
Baseball star appears,
one hundred and one courageous kids

I Want to Watch the Mets Game!

I want to watch the Mets play
in the fields of America,
Mets play in town squares,
I want to watch the Mets game!

When I'm driving my car
I want street signs to read:
"Over the right field wall, It's outta here!"
I want to watch the Mets game!

Officer, Officer
when you stopped me last night
why did you ask for my license, registration
and insurance card,
instead of a parking ticket
give me a ticket to the ballpark,
I want to watch the Mets game!

When I'm on a date,
don't patronize me with mascara, good looks
tell me about, Kingman, Seaver and Hubie Brooks
I want to watch the Mets game!

When we're at the restaurant
don't push today's special on me,
just serve up an entrée
of Amazin` Cuisine
a platter of Beltran, a side of Endy,
Piazza, Thornberry, Zeile Parmesan
a plate of Strawberry Teufel

Pedro con Carne, Cherry Koosman Cheese Cake,
Grilled Rack of Wendell, extra rare!
I want to watch the Mets game!

When I'm watching TV
don't tell me about the economy,
war, greed and politics,
tell me about contracts,
acquisitions and starting lineups,
I want to watch the Mets game!

When the commercials come on,
don't tell me it's better in the Bahamas
Yes, I know it's been a long winter,
and I could use a rest,
just give me my team the New York Mets,
I want to watch the Mets game!

Soldier Haiku

Soldier at the game
National Anthem is played,
single tear-drop falls

Bone Man and Mets Poet in Memphis

Bone Man fires up the Charger
adorning horn-rimmed shades,
long white beard of angels,
heads to Memphis
to meet the Mets Poet
for Civil Rights Game 2008

Bone Man is from Kentucky,
home of Pee Wee Reese
and the Louisville Slugger,
Mets Poet is from New Jersey,
home of baseball's birth
and Jackie's first pro-game

Bone Man arrives at the Peabody
with five bucks in change, a fiery grin
and electricity in his boots,
Mets Poet arrives with two tickets
to the ballgame and a dream
of celebrating American hero MLK

Bone Man and Mets Poet
visit Civil Rights Museum
where so many lives changed
America changed, Bone Man
still heavy-hearted with memories of '68
came here soon after MLK was shot

Bone Man stood in the same spot,
alone, a young man

now forty years later with the Mets Poet,
a ramshackle Lorraine Motel
turned "Grand Central Station"
of the civil rights movement

Bone Man adjusts weary eyes,
strokes long white beard of angels,
looks out from balcony
with the rain pouring down,
points crooked finger
toward the soul of America
and yells "Never give up,
no matter what is going on.
Never give up!"

9/21/01 (for Mike Piazza)

From the late-night hours of September 11, 2001
through September 14, I volunteered along with hun-
dreds of others in the aftermath of the terrorist attacks.
At Exchange Place in Jersey City, I loaded food and sup-
plies that were being ferried directly across the river to
the World Trade Center site.

New Jersey Governor Jon S. Corzine and Sena-
tor Robert Torricelli spoke at the foot of Grand Street,
greeted and thanked the volunteers. One of the staffers
handed out ticket vouchers redeemable for the next ball
game at Shea Stadium. In the midst of this horrific loss,
who was thinking about baseball? It seemed insignifi-
cant and far away; the furthest thing from my mind.
Besides, the season was officially put on hold.

I gazed across the river into a fog of dust and bone,
and suddenly it clicked. That simple piece of paper is a
symbol of hope. The nation will rise, the city will heal,
and the games will once again be played. I wiped my
brow, reached out my hand and accepted the ticket.

On September 21, 2001, Mets baseball returned to
New York City. I grabbed the ticket, started my car and
headed to the game.

As I approached the Fort Lee toll plaza, I was
greeted by armed National Guards. I thought about the
friends and family I had asked to join me. They were
skittish. Security would be tight, too much anxiety, not
sure if it's appropriate. All the excuses were legitimate.
As I drove across the George Washington Bridge, I could
see lower Manhattan smoldering in the distance. The
burning electrical smell permeated the interior of my

car. I sighed, knowing fate would have me attend this game alone.

I could see the horror all around me, but I couldn't believe it. Nervous glances of shell-shocked commuters, the screams of fighter jets overhead. It was like getting through a moat of bad energy, sorrow, disbelief and death.

On the other hand, drivers were noticeably polite. No honking, no obscene gestures. Even the cab drivers extended rights-of-way on a bottled-necked Grand Central Parkway.

As I rounded the bend past LaGuardia Airport, Shea came into view like an old friend. The lights glittered over the stadium like a cathedral during Christmas time, a holy place, a womb of protection from the cruel world that surrounded us.

I parked in my usual spot, on the grassy island between the 112th St. service road and Flushing Bay, beneath the humming overpass of Northern Boulevard. I've parked there for fifteen years, one hop of the curb and you're there. Free, accessible and an easy escape route.

I turned the car off, took a deep breath and peered into the rear-view mirror. Staring back at me was the face of a rattled man. Pupils dilated, uncertainty, grief. I adjusted the faded blue cap on my head, tapped the mirror three times and said out loud to the man in the reflection, "Just go enjoy yourself. Don't worry."

As I walked through the parking lot, most every car had a flag pointing to high heaven. Someone handed out small stars and stripes on sticks. "Made in the USA," she proclaimed. I mounted Old Glory into my left shirt pocket and continued through the masses. Families walked hand-in-hand, fathers and sons played catch, barbecues glowed.

The voice of WFAN's Eddie Coleman echoed from a car radio. Mets against Braves, right here at Shea Stadium.

Yes, baseball had returned to New York.

I settled in along the third base line, Section 118. The pre-game ceremony was poignant, honorable and at times, gut wrenching. Members of the FDNY, EMT, NYPD and the PAPD participated in the on-field ceremony in their fresh uniforms, but you could sense the pain emanating from the postures of these fine men and women. Planes flew loud and low as they usually do over Shea Stadium. However, with the roars came the cruel reminder of what had occurred only ten days prior.

Mayor Rudy Giuliani was welcomed as a hero by the Shea faithful. At that moment, the city and country was unified in unprecedented fashion. The moment of silence was followed by the saddest, most beautiful bagpipe rendition of "America the Beautiful". Diana Ross sang "God Bless America". Ceremonial first pitches were thrown by rescue workers, then a joyous Star Spangled Banner was sung by Marc Anthony. The loud and hearty chants of "U-S-A" bellowed from the stands in perfect unison.

By the time Mets starter Bruce Chen threw the first pitch, some of the anxiety and uncertainty had dissipated. The Mets and Braves started off playing a timid game of baseball, each team reluctant to break the ice of competition.

However, as usual, the Braves struck first, with arch-nemesis Chipper Jones crossing the plate in the fourth inning. "Lar-ry, Lar-ry!" chanted the crowd.

The Mets tied the game in the bottom of the fourth where it remained until the eighth inning. During the seventh inning stretch, Liza Minelli sang a spirited and lively version of "New York, New York", flanked by members of the FDNY and NYPD.

Although there was an uneasiness about the game, I really wanted the Mets to win. As the Braves managed to scrape the go-ahead run in the top of the eighth inning, the level of sadness and excitement shifted back and forth like a cruel tide. My eyes pinned to the red, white and blue bow that was placed over the spot where the Twin Towers stood in the mock skyline atop the outfield scoreboard.

The score of the game was 2-1, bottom of the eighth. Steve Karsay in relief for the Braves. Mike Piazza lumbered to the plate in his usual stoic, immovable fashion. Two, three practice swings, a glance to the plate, then back at a focused Steve Karsay.

Mike swung. The crack of the bat was met by 41,235 of the loudest and raucous cheers I've ever heard in my life. Mike sent the ball over the left-center field wall and along with it, our grief. Shea Stadium seemed to levitate with emotion. I hugged a stranger, then another. Unified by country, city, the game of baseball. Our team. The New York Mets.

The tears that flowed from our faces were joyous, poignant tears. Mike Piazza had saved us, for a moment. A moment we desperately needed. The city desperately needed. Humanity desperately needed.

The win was secured with Armando Benitez closing it out. I left Shea Stadium, walked to my car, which was waiting for me in that same familiar spot it's been waiting after each game for the past fifteen years. I turned the car on, took a deep breath, then peered into the rear-view mirror. Staring back at me was a man with hope in his eyes. I adjusted the faded blue cap on my head, tapped the mirror three times and said out loud to the man in the reflection, "I know everything will be all right. I know *everything* will be all right!"

Part VI
Foul Ball

Philly Lou

Lou's my bartender,
local tavern, personalized mug
beer's cold, patrons warm

One problem, Lou's a Philly fan
red hats, red buttons, red Ps
hidden between bottles, wine glasses,
a staged battle of superstition and luck

One day, stopped in,
rearranged Lou's gadgets,
switched the hats around
and wished his team bad habits

It didn't work...yet

Ticket Stub

I open desk drawer to get a stamp,
post office closing in twenty-minutes, hurry up

bottom falls out, assorted items fall,
annals of junk drawer history

damn Ikea piece of shit!

throw keys down, remove jacket
sort through mysterious mess:

Erasers, matches, hand sanitizer,
cigarette lighter, subway token,
enough pens to supply a family of nerds,
prescription bottle, Bazooka Joe comic,

Directions to John's house, black button,
half a credit card, screwdriver, Vick's vapor inhaler,
Scotch tape, another half a credit card,
ticket stubs, dozens and dozens of Mets ticket stubs!

Pick one up, May 10, 1996
another game, another memory,
another folded, dog-eared ticket stub
till I turn it over, a phone number

then it clicked:

Tommy and his wife, Carol:
saw them at game, small talk

how's the kids, life is good, nice to see you

Tommy in a Rico Brogna jersey,
his wife, an Ordonez t-shirt
ranting, raving, things look good,
couple of trades, playoffs, who knows

I shuffle through the junk,
thinking about Tommy, grade school
Mets t-shirt but a Yankee cap,
What a confused, strange bird

Still, childhood school chum
middle age Mets fan, not a bad guy
just for kicks, dial the number

Same number, same house, different wife
one kid, fifth grade, the older one in high school

"How'd you like to hit the game Tommy?"

"Sure," he says. "You got tickets?"

"Season, third base line, Friday night, let's go!"

"Wait! Impossible!"

"They're not playing home Friday, they're in Boston!"

"What?"

"The Yankees, they're playing in Boston, not New York!"

"I have Mets tickets, not Yanks, we're Mets fans."

"Hey shit-head" he hollered, "I'm a Yankee fan, you
should know that. You've known
me since fifth grade. Yanks fan!"

"Well, what the hell
were you doing at a Mets game
on May 10, 1996
wearing a Rico Brogna jersey,
your wife an Ordonez shirt,
picture of your son with a Mets cap
on his head?"

"Shut up, you're an idiot!"

"You don't want to go to the game on Friday, fine. Just
make sure your kid doesn't take after his old man
by wearing a *Mets t-shirt* on his *body* and a *Yankee cap*
on his *head!*
Twenty years later go to a *Mets game* with a *Rico
Brogna jersey!*
Only to find out, he's really a *Yankee fan!*
You're an abomination *to the sport of baseball* and
should be banned from *every stadium in the world!*"

The line goes dead

I reassemble drawer,
replace the junk and push it closed,

out flutters a single stamp, a butterfly,
I catch it, lick, press to envelope
Post office closing, ten minutes, hurry up,
down Grand Street, cross Washington
squirrel in my path, gets on hind legs,
juggles acorns, speaks a language I understand

Still thinking about Tommy

Well, what can you do?
Not everyone can be as normal as me

Chrissy the Waitress Gets Fired

Chrissy the waitress bounced her way toward me,
an inflated, friendly beach toy

What would you like, Frank? The usual?

Come to game with me tomorrow
Mets-Yanks, subway series under the sun,
you know?

Face lit up, lights turned on,
Are you serious? I'd love to go!

Pick you up at four o'clock?

Perfect, see you tomorrow!

Paid my check, left the bar
waved through the plate-glass window
her face glowing, a million-dollar smile

Next day, 4 o'clock, pick her up,
Mets cap on her head, same million-dollar smile

We discuss important things:
baseball, baseball and baseball,
her cell phone rings

What's the matter?

That was my boss, supposed to work tonight or get fired,
sweet smile momentarily chased away

Didn't you request the day off?
Personal day, call in sick, something

Told them the truth, subway series
Mets and Yanks under the sun, you know?

Apology to a Television Set

You have withstood
long years of physical and verbal abuse
inflicted by my own hands, tossed shoes, beer cans
Chinese food containers
and
there were times I kicked and cursed,
hoisted you over my shoulder
and tossed you through the window
but
you came back
delivering me good news;
how great the team was doing,
how it was only a matter of time
we'd clinch the division
but
one night, with my mouth
stuffed with beer, pastrami and vulgarity
I once again turned on you,
hoisted you over my shoulder
and tossed you through the window
but
this time you were taken away by another man
who tossed you into the back of a garbage truck,
taking you to a place where broken dreams,
failed seasons and abused television sets
are buried for eternity

Two Fouls

Look at me, Look at me
I caught a foul ball,
my moment of glory,
see me holding ball?

Look at me, look at me
I caught a foul ball,
look at me standing,
Was I on TV?

With envy they stare,
my dream, not theirs!
but as I revel, look down at my hands,
the ball it rolls down a system of stairs

Into the hands of an eight-year-old fan,
who runs, cheers, gallops and leaps,
pokes my eye and gladly screams,

"Look at me, look at me,
I caught a foul ball,
my moment of glory,
see me holding ball!"

New Television Set! (9/13/07)

You're very lucky!
The salesman from Sears
bolted you to the wall
and said it would take
a very strong and angry person
to rip you off the hinges,
I think you'll be around a while,
After all, we are seven games ahead of the Phillies
with only seventeen games left to play

To a Common Fan (Whitman Revisited)

Be disheveled, be uneasy with me, I am Frank Messina, arrogant and
cantankerous as any fan you'll meet
Not till the final out excludes you, do I exclude you
Not till the rain refuses to annoy you and the loudmouths
rustle with you, do I refuse to annoy and rustle you
My fan, I disappoint you with a disappointment, and I charge that you
make no hesitation to disappoint me
And I charge that you be impatient and imperfect till victory comes
Till then I tip my cap to you with a significant look that you do not forget me

Fouled Up

D and I at the game,
two seats empty by our side,
our friends they must be late

Behind us, three silver-haired gals
scorecard, programs and hats

D snuggles closer, we take in the sight
green grass, light breeze, summer night

First inning, foul ball, just beyond my reach,
ball knocked by the silver-haired
stuck firmly beneath their seats

I reach and grab with all my might
The ball I got to my delight

I hold the ball and bask in glory
then I hear a silver-haired story:

"Years of coming close but never getting the ball."
Faces of disappointment, silver-haired and all

I turn, hand them the fouled off gem,
filled with memories of the moment

The gals they giggled and smiled a smile
of three little girls with silver hair

D and I at the game,

two seats empty by our side
our friends they must be late

I check our tickets once again, bang my hand to head
"Wrong section, wrong seats," the silver-haired said!

Blinded by Love of Game

Again, the beauty comes,
to congregations,
the church of pastime,
timeless, love abounds, again
D in the night, with a pounding heart,
beating breast, tearing me apart,
limb by limb, till next lover balks

Again, the beauty comes,
whispers its song on spring mornings,
crack of the bat, smell the leather,
taste the glory again,
summer shady citrus tree, bearing fruit
for one hundred and sixty two sunsets
till love carries me home again
and I become blinded by the love of game

One Day

One day
all world leaders
came to play
a baseball game

The people gathered
in the stands,
to cheer their leaders on

The leaders
took the field with their gloves,
bats and balls

The game they played
wasn't pretty,
walks, balks and lots of errors
while others hit home-runs

At the end of the game
the world leaders protested and complained
who won? who's to blame?
but the world's people
came and watched
and the people won the game!

Lost in Atlantic City

My entire life, a crapshoot,
a spin of the wheel, a royal flush,
decisions circling in my head, a ball
running counter-clockwise
to the roulette wheel

Ball drops,
I collect my chips, cash them in
for steak, red wine
ball game on bar room TV
ninth inning, Lidge against Wright
full count, cards dealt
slot machine arm pulled
wheel spins, ball falls into slot

My number called, my time is up
I move on to a place
with a pocket full of chips,
a shit-eating grin
and a dream
that will never die

Part VII
In the Stands

Idiot with Cell Phone Becomes Hero in Wild Walk-Off Win

A man stands,
one hand waving
to someone, somewhere
other hand to ear, cell phone
"see me in the stands,
that's me waving!"

A woman stands,
one hand waving
to someone, somewhere
other hand to ear, cell phone
"see me in the stands,
that's me waving!"

A man stands,
waving to someone, somewhere
"see me waving?"

Another man stands, takes cell phone,
throws from stands to first base

Jason Giambi picks up phone,
puts to ear, "Who is this?"
"It's Freddy, I'm in the stands,
see me waving my hand?"

Wright hits a line-drive,
past Giambi,
two runs score, Mets win!

Agnes

She's at every game
black sweater sleeves rolled up
red lipstick, faded blue cap on dyed black hair,
fidgeting digits tapping the armrest
with each pitch, inning, game, season
there is Agnes
never cheering, never standing
just watching and waiting
checking scoreboard
then back to the mound and to the scoreboard again,
nipping fingertips,
Pulling napkin from sweater pocket,
back in, then out again
watching, waiting, biting lip, wringing hands
with an occasional glance to her seated neighbors
then snapping back to the game,
Once, between innings,
Agnes and I made eye contact
and in that moment
I saw a world of uncertainty
flash from her eyes;
a mother waiting for a child
or a friend who will not arrive

The Last Mets Hammer Ever Sold at Shea

The concession stand
orange and blue
had Mets hammers for sale

I bought one

Took it to my seat
and waved it over my head,
with each strike that whizzed
by the plate, a cheerful
"Hey Chipper, chop this!" I said

The new "judge" in the stands,
stainless steel gavel in hand,
the dazzled fans, "ahh'd" and "ooo'd"
where'd you get such a durable tool?

George the Security Man soon arrived,
puzzled how I smuggled, then flaunted
a carpenter's hammer before his eyes

Told him I bought it,
"Here's my receipt.
See, one hammer, twenty-five dollars
paid in cash at 9:25"

Realizing the silly scenario
George the Security Man let me go,
on condition he retain the mallet of menace
till after the game, to which I gladly said, "yes"

When George the Security Man
later handed over the tool,
he shook my hand, congratulated and said,
"That's the last Mets hammer ever sold at Shea!"

Irv the Concession Man

I buy a round of eight-dollar beers
from Irv the Concession Man,
hand him the money, he pours

IDs out everyone, IDs out!

I take my beers, step aside

A gray-haired man with a walker
and an oxygen tank shuffles forward

Give me a beer, sonny!

IDs out everyone, IDs out!

The old man, points to his ear,
shakes head, hands Irv ten bucks,
motions to keep the change

IDs out everyone! IDs out!

I head toward my seat,
the old man with the walker
strolling in front of me,
a mile-wide grin on his face

Play Ball!

Psycho Chick Goes to the Ball Park

I was in my seat for less than a minute
when she appeared from the park's dark corner

the psycho chick

she grabbed my lapels,
kissed hand, nibbled ears,
whispered stories of Eva Perón
Yoga, and the joy of handcuffs

We made our way to the Diamond Club,
drank red wine
sucked face, necks and pinkies for a while,
then went to the car, lot 12c
steamed up the windows
and kissed goodbye

Three days later
I committed the horrible crime
of calling her back
for more handcuffs and more Eva Perón

I told her she was a nice girl
that I enjoyed her company,
after cutting through the small talk,
we agreed to meet again

me and the psycho chick

I took her to the ballgame

bought drinks, dogs and snacks
we were the perfect couple,
ushers tipped their caps,
beer vendors called me "lucky man"

But, it wasn't too long
before the psycho chick
began to laugh wildly,
flicking peanuts at three
large men in the stands
I told her it wasn't polite to do that,
they'll take it as an act of disrespect
and start trouble with me,
At Shea Stadium,
when you throw peanuts
at three large men,
they don't bother calling security

She rolled her eyes
flicked another peanut
and told me I was pathetic

She reached toward my middle
and slowly squeezed
until I was blue in the face

Then from her purse
she pulled out a lipstick
scribbling words on my forehead
then,
the Kiss-cam caught us by surprise

and there I was on the big screen
with the words "Mets Suck" scribbled on my face

The crowd booed,
peanuts were tossed, beers thrown,
three large men approached,
old women clubbed me with canes
children stuck bubble gum to my hair,
so I pointed to the Psycho Chick
but
she rubbed her palms and clicked her heels,
and crept back to the park's dark corner

The game finished, the pitcher bowed
then he crept to the park's dark corner,
oblivious to the impending doom awaiting him
in the form of

the psycho chick

The Outsider

One day, the poet went to a reading
and all the cynics were there
exchanging metaphor, simile, hyperbole
through the stench of clove-filled air

After the reading, they gargled on words;
words of a narrow, political tone,
with mouths agape, they ranted and raved
scratched their goatees and tugged their berets

With bushy eyebrows, fangs and teeth,
they blamed everyone else for their own grief
like the tea in their cups, they winced and became
bitter, boring, oversteeped and deranged

The poet, he trembled then ran for the door
his eyes and his ears could take it no more
instead to the game, he fled with his glove
to see pure poetry; the game that he loved

Three Strikes, three outs, nine men, nine frames
where the poet sees beauty, others see shame
they laugh and they holler, "what a waste of time!"
the poet alone, pens nine-inning rhymes

Brad

His face is a catcher's mitt
turned inside out;
leather cheeks held together
by a support strap system
of wrinkled steerhide

His jersey reads
"I need help!"
but his face screams, "It's too late!"

On Sunday mornings
over Bloody Marys and Lox,
Brad makes small talk with waitresses
and quips back to their "Lets go Mets!" greetings
with "Why, where they going?"

Stirring his drink with a celery stalk
Brad describes being a fan
as a form of voluntary torture
that offers few rewards, if any

Once, through the grovel
of a smoker's rasp
Brad told me a story
of how a hundred men
leapt to their deaths
after a Benitez-blown-save
yet
through the heaviness of his lids
I saw a hundred Brads, celery stalks in hand
leaping at the ready

Tattoo Man

The game has found its way
under his skin
permeated, needled, branded
on burly limbs

Biceps flex, Mr. Met smiles,
Calf muscle shifts, Seaver tosses,
Shea swells from shoulder blades
in vintage orange and blue

Inked, baked, sun-weary skin
a mural of colored wounds;
a life festooned in triumph
and a body scarred by glory

Dr. Doom the Dentist

Dr. Doom, the dentist;
drills teeth by day
cheers Mets by night
cavities, injections, root canals
witness of agony, 9-5
tooth aches, drill, injections, suction
drill, suction, spit, rinse
chipped molars, metallic flavor
Novocain, sweet air, spit, suction
drill, suction, spit, rinse
but
at night
it's his turn in the chair

With a grimace
he watches and waits
tugging at the brim of his cap
closing eyes as the ball is released
from pitcher's hand
suction, spit, injection, drill
wincing, whining, clutching arms of chair
suction, spit, drill,
tap-tap-tap
drill-drill-drill

-rinse-

"it's not enough to have a seven-run lead
we need more runs!"

suction, drill, tap-tap, drill, suction, spit, rinse

"Hit it forward, Hit it forward!"
"Stop prancing like a ballerina!"
"You should be given a lethal injection, you bum!"

tap-tap, drill, suction, spit, rinse, drill-drill-drill
is it safe? drill-drill-drill

"No, he was out!"

Drill-drill-drill,
suction, spit, rinse
tap-tap-tap, drill-drill-drill

"The guy is a bum! We're gonna lose!"
we need more, more, more, we need more!"

Drill-drill-drill, suction, spit, rinse
suction, spit rinse, drill-drill-drill

Dr. Doom has become one
with his chair, relenting
-a poster child for agony-
finally the game ends
his team wins, cavities filled, no more pain
and
tomorrow
Dr. Doom will try to keep a steady hand
as he greets early morning patients
with a grin and the buzz of a dentist's drill

tap-tap-tap
drill-drill-drill
injection, suction, spit, rinse

Usher

Luke wears a purple heart
on his hat, earned during World War II
twisted digits scan the ticket
squints bespectacled eyes
then leads us to a place where we
lay our own eyes upon;
a field of green with nine men
battling a glorious battle
toward October's dream
and
the same eyes that saw men fall
in other glorious battles
now find refuge and peace
in a place where the masses celebrate
but
as the curtain closes on this old Shea
My concern turns to Luke and his crew;
what yielded interest awaits them
when the sun shines on Citi Field?
What twisted digits, what bespectacled eyes
shall lead us to our newfound home?

Bubble Junk

Scorecard collection,
remove one from shelf

August 10, 1988, Mets-Cardinals

Pages stuck together with bubble gum

What the shit man! Who put gum in my program?

Then it clicked:

D and I at the game,
satanic little devil
blowing bright, red bubbles
snapping away behind us

I went to the toilet, then a beer

Came back, kid and his parents gone, thank God

Twenty years later
I find bright red bubble junk
and
that kid, now twenty-eight or thirty,
behind a desk, running a company,
a lawyer
or maybe a dentist
making a decent salary,
probing mouths
for bright, red bubble gum,

thinking of that rotten man
he annoyed way back in 1988
by sticking gum
between the sheets
of his scorecard

Cotton Candy Face

Little blue devil
sticky face, sticky hands,
wanders to our seats,
stickies up the stands

Little blue devil
sticky face and hands,
grinning demonic, blue-devil grin

Little blue devil
sticky face, sticky hands,
wanders to our seats,
stickies up the stands

Little blue devil
sticky face and hands
your little cotton candy face
is starting to annoy me

Little blue devil
pointing blue sugar-digits at me,
parents, won't you please
come take him away from me?

Shuffling Shaw

I took Shuffling Shaw to the game,
first inning, out for a smoke

Second inning, searched under seat,
lost keys, wallet, told him they're
in his own two hands

"Oh," he said, scratched his head
then he watched the game

I took Shuffling Shaw to the game
he shuffled, tussled couldn't get comfy

Beer man comes, Heineken or Bud?
Shaw he grumbled, groaned and shuffled

"I don't know what I want."

Beer man cracks two Buds
hands them to Shuffling Shaw,
he shuffles, gruffles, grunts and groans
then he watched the game

Carla the Cleaning Lady

She chooses targets wisely
broken pretzel, mustard packets
scooped into her magic sweeper tool

Casualties discarded by clumsy fans
popcorn, napkins, soda cans
consumed by her hungry gadget

A man drops a five-dollar bill
on the sticky concourse floor
Carla scoops it up, hands it to the man

The man thumbs his beard
then begrudgingly inquires
wasn't that a ten I dropped?

Timmy the Ticket Taker

Timmy the Ticket Taker's
been taking tickets
since '66
topping the record
for taking tickets
from ticketed ticketees
since the mid-sixties

Timmy the Ticket taker
told me Tuesday he once took a ticket
from a guy named Tippy the Trippy,
on a date with Tina the Tipsy

Timmy the Ticket Taker took the ticket
from Tippy the Trippy and
asked Tina the Tipsy for her ticket,
but Tina the Tipsy took too long
so Tippy the Trippy entered alone

Tina the Tipsy ticked off and sighed,
Timmy the Ticket Taker said, "Please don't cry!"
Timmy the Ticket Taker and Tina the Tipsy
soon fell in love
and now live happily ever after
as Mr. and Mrs. Timmy and Tina
the Tipsy Ticket Takers

Cowbell Man

Have you seen Cowbell Man
with his jersey, cap and bell?

He walks up and down the aisles
and celebrates the Mets

Clunk-clunk-clunk! he clunks
with an old drumstick

Clunk-clunk-clunk! he clunks
and the fans join in

Have you heard Cowbell Man
with his jersey, cap and bell?

You don't have to be at the game
to hear his clunk-clunk bell

Just tune in to TV or radio
and if you listen carefully,
you'll hear the sound of Cowbell Man
clunk-clunk-clunking his Mets toward victory!

Benny the Balancing Beer Man

Have you seen Benny the Beer Man
balancing a case of beer on his head?

He hawks the suds up and down the aisle,
"Beer here, hey beer!" the fans all smile

Benny the Beer Man with beers and ales
the better he balances, the better his sales

The more you drink the more you'll think
Benny the Beer Man belongs in "the clink"

Millie

For years Millie served me drinks, dogs and fries
She proudly wore Mets hat, pins and ties

"Let's go Mets," she said, with a smile and a grin
I'd tip her every time, Millie at the concession bin

One day the Mets played "on the other side of town,"
I arrived with my Mets gear, politely bought a round

Lo and behold, old Millie there, adorned in "other" wear
"Millie, oh Millie, how can this be? Why have you forsaken me?"

Kenny the Kangaroo

Hopping, leaping, bouncing
to his seat for first pitch

Kenny the Kangaroo
tap-tap-taps
impatiently,
his giant sneaker-feet,
swiveling ears
with each crack-crack-crack
of the bat-bat-bat
Kenny the Kangaroo

Big brown eyes
above his snout,
follow play-by-play,
balancing on his tail
when a foul ball comes his way

Captain Konstantin

He's elated as easily
as he is deflated,
win, lose, win,
there is Konstantin
defiant, against all odds,
rising with the team
unafraid to sink with the ship

a captain!

Freddy the Fair-Weathered Fan

At the game, Giants and Mets
San Fran up, one-nothing,
Freddy wears number twenty-five,

Bonds jersey

Freddy cheers, arms raised
big smile, proudly turns
pointing to shirt,

Bonds jersey

Home-run, Mets up three-to-one
Freddy's eyes swing left to right,
slowly unbuttons his

Bonds jersey

Mets clobber three more,
Freddy squirms, slinks out of the shirt
underneath it, a brand new

METS jersey

At the game, Giants and Mets
San Fran down, nine-to-one,
Freddy the fair-weathered fan
stuffs something under his chair:

Bonds jersey!

Wrong Seats

They wander, ticket stubs in hand
scratching heads, disoriented

searching through a maze of letters, numbers

down in front, sit down!

finally they sit, somewhere, anywhere
members of the lost and found

ten minutes later, three more wanderers,
my seats, you're in my seats!

no, these are ours, see, here's my ticket

down in front, sit down!

finally, the disoriented concede, leave
and the wanderers take their seats

three rows over, members of the lost and found
continue searching through a maze of letters, numbers

down in front, sit down! down in front! Sit down!

The Heckler

Every game the heckler yells
to the opposing right fielder,
"It's going over your head!"

Every team, every game, he heckles,

"Winn, it's going over your head!"
"Over your head Hermida, over your head!"
"Nady, over your head, move out Nady!"

It's not working Mr. Heckler, sit down!

The heckler sits down, hands folded, not a word

Beltran hits one over his head!

Dr. Doom

A shy, hungry giant
lumbers through the stands,
clutching box of chicken nuggets

Dr. Doom!

He gravitates, center of seat
shoulders unhinged, head in hands,
a convict awaiting sentence

Dr Doom tugs brim of cap,
pitcher releases ball, the giant screams,
"Seven runs ain't enough, we need more runs!"

pops another nugget into mouth

"The guy is a bum! We need more, more,
we need more!"

two, three, four nuggets into mouth
two, three, four runs cross plate

Mets up, eleven to three, bottom of the eighth
but he screams, "Hit the ball, hit the ball,
you should be kicked and beaten
and your hair lit on fire!"

two, three, four nuggets into mouth
one, two, three outs, Mets win!

Dr. Doom exhales, wipes mouth,
rises, lumbers through stands,
traffic, trains, lays hard head on soft pillow

but tomorrow

Dr. Doom will again
lumber through stands, clutching nuggets
and remain through nine innings,
imprisoned by the incessant desire to win

Part VIII
Again, the Signs

Dad at Sloan-Kettering,
He's Got Something to Tell Me

The sun through his window,
a swollen heart

"Got the newspaper Dad, and black licorice too."

No answer, a gentle, rhythmic snore

I pull the armchair closer
ease into it softly, gently, not a sound

I study jaundiced face and hands
remembering what he said:

there's not much time

Touch his feet, wrapped in white blanket,
I gaze out the window

A single white bird circled over the East River,
an angel, then disappear into clouds

Throat tightens, lips tremble
A teardrop caught in the palm of my hand

He awakes, motions, whispers, "Come here."
I wipe tears from my eyes, move to his side

"Come closer," he says, "I've got something to tell you.
Heart sinks to stomach, what's he got to tell me now?

I move closer, lean in and listen
to him slowly gently whisper the words,

"You were the only planned one!"

The Impossible Dream (for Bob Murphy)

It was a sad, beautiful day
when Bob Murphy said goodbye,
hand held high, wife by his side
we stood, cheered, cried,
chills up and down our spine

Recollecting, as a child
hearing Murph call the plays,
a friendly, intonated voice
hovering my youthful days

Bob Murphy, a soundtrack
of my youth; voice reaching out
through backyard, stickball
through sprinklers, hydrants
and pushing me ever so gently
toward and realizing the impossible dream

Civil Rights Game Haiku

Two bards in Memphis
forty years, nine innings since,
black bird free at last

Mets Fan

I'm a second-class citizen
trapped in a first-rate city
son of a Brooklyn-Dodging-Giant,
laid to rest in the back-alleys of Muttsville

I'm a Mets fan!

I'm the beat, the outsider;
Slumbering through broken dreams
like an abandoned umbrella, blowing
down Big Apple's Broadway
of "meaningless September"

I'm a Mets fan!

I've been yanked,
drag-bunted, tossed to the corner dive-bar
looking for solace in a static-ridden TV
sipping beer, waiting for glory
in the bottom of the ninth;
the miracle RBI that never comes,
but never goes away
always believing, always believing,
because

I'm a Mets fan!

I've been rejected
by the "Canyon of Heroes" for way too long
been ejected from the Back Page for way too long

been wishing for a wild card for way too long
believing in Miracles for way too long
instead
replaying the tapes of '86
replaying the tapes of '86
"and it gets through Buckner's legs"
for way too long

I'm a Mets fan

I'm tired of banging my head against the wall
calling WFAN through long, hot summers
chatting with Steve Somers
shmoozing and consoling,
"Hey, it's alright to dream," because

I'm a Mets fan

When my team loses
I get the deep, dark, bluesy, blues
but
when the Metropolitans
pull out a win by the skin of their cleats
You'll see me dancing in the streets
Buying drinks for all around
yes, even for our friends from the other side of town
Yes, I'm a maniacal Metropolitan Mets fan
I'm a Let-Go-Mets-Go-Mets-Go-Fan
I'm an M-E-T-S New York Mets fan

I'm a Mets fan!

Meat Grinder

I have found
the perfect companion
to watch Mets games with:

-a meat grinder-

At the start of each game
I place the grinder next to my chair
crack a beer, recline and let the fun begin

First I place my fingers
into the chute and dangle them
over the spinning blades

With each passing inning
my fingers move deeper into the machine
until I feel the pressure of the blades
against my fingertips

At first, I ignore the pain
it's just a few lacerations, that's all
and besides, we're leading
by a score of "three-zip" in the eighth

but, then a pitching change
and it's Aaron Heilman

I start to get a sick feeling

My fingers become lodged

beyond return, then my forearm

I lean forward in the chair
shaking left to right
hoping to free myself from the
stainless steel beast now dangling
from the side of my body

Heilman walks
leadoff man in four pitches
and I start sinking
deeper into the machine

I push back from the chair
lifting right leg over head
then down against the meat grinder
trying to force loose
but
my foot slips into the chute
then calf, knee and thigh

With one leg left, I furiously
kick at the meat grinder
yet it too becomes lodged and devoured

Now, head and torso
sticking out of the chute;
my other half being
pressed out of the grinder plates

-I begin to panic-

Then it happens:
Heilman gives up another walk
a base hit, then a home run

-another blown game-

Down I go,
forced through the bowels
of a meat grinder,
pressed through chute and blades,
and onto the floor
in a glorious, warm and bleeding
pile of fan bits

I am Finished

I am finished in the aisles of Shea
cheering a team that will never bring
my old man back from the grave
I am finished flirting with the gals
who hickeyed their way back to my apartment
and flaunted their firm breasts toward the moonlight
as I squeezed their buttocks at eighteen

I am finished sipping from waterlogged cups
whose beer drips and drabs into my lap
as I stare down opposing pitchers
wishing jinxes on their athletic bods
I am finished drinking the night away until
a good poem finds its way to this swollen heart
I am finished beating my head against the wall

I am finished believing in you and all the dreams
that died their slow, September death
I am done eating you out, busting my balls
bleeding on the Brooklyn-Queens Expressway
with each murder on the field of Old Shea
why, why must I bear this torment
where's the way out of this false hope, this illusion
this relentless torture chamber of self-inflicted wounds

Life is a Baseball Game

Conception is Spring training
birth, opening day

April is childhood
May, adolescence

June is adulthood
July, middle age

August is senior adulthood
September is sundown

and if you're lucky

There's always October

10/18

Gorgeous October night
entire family at game,
brothers, sister, nephew in Loge,
mother and I in Field

Dad's seventieth, had he lived
on this glorious day at Shea,
but Mom and I, and Dad above
celebrate our team, family,
in the home we love
and love is all that matters

The Home Run Apple

Over the years
she brought smiles
and in exchange, cheers
with a simple rise
from center field

The Home Run Apple

She wasn't shiny, a bit shabby
but she rose up, most of the time
and if not, her eyes poked out
from black hat where she lived

The Home Run Apple

Mets Montage

Family, friends
city skyline, setting sun
Casey, Gil, Thornberry,
World's Fair, the Fab Four

#7 Train, Seaver, Ryan, Jones
black cat circling, Cubs and Cards
Canyon of Heroes, the Miracle
Orange, blue, green, red seats

The roar! jet planes overhead
The roar! Loyal orange and blue
The roar! Kingman arching one deep

Banner day!

The roar! Strawberry over the right field wall
The roar! Nails, Mex, Hojo and Backman
The roar! Mookie Wilson, Knight around third

The roar! Piazza lifts the city with one swing
The roar! He rounds third, the roar, the roar, the roar!
Endy's leaping grab, The roar!

Doggy Day at Shea!

The roar! LoDuca nails two at the plate
The roar! José triples, slides and smiles
The roar! Wright rounds third, tying the score

The roar! a gorgeous walk-off win
The roar! Beltran does it again
The roar! Delgado comes alive

Last Play at Shea

The roar! Shea closes its doors
The roar! We enter Citi Field
The roar! The roar! The roar!

Family, friends, mother, father,
sister, brother, children, grandparents,

A high foul ball into the stands
sting of the ball in the palm of your hands!

The Roar! The Roar! The Roar!

Mad Dog Blues

Listen to you whine
from dirty, doggy throne
the Giants been swept, ole dog
you flea-infested hound

Mad dog, oh Mad Dog
the Mets swept your Giants
and all a mad dog can do
is whine, whine, whine

My Mets done clean up house
Giants leave in shame
I tune to your show on F.A.N.
you whine all afternoon

Mad dog, oh Mad dog
the Mets swept your Giants
and all a mad dog can do
is whine, whine, whine

Oh I love to hear Mad Dog,
bang his head against the wall,
for years, you put my team down
now your tail between your legs

Mad Dog, Oh Mad Dog
go back to your dirty, doggy throne
the Mets swept your Giants home
now go and leave me alone

On '86

Do you remember '86?
I mean, do you *really* remember?

Yes, I remember quite well

The Cold War was in full bloom,
Reagan was President
and Keith Hernandez was God

I was eighteen-years-old
and we die-hard Messina's
had season tickets, third base line

Everyone wants to talk about Crazy Game Six
but there were 108 regular season wins
that led to the magical, inevitable October

Seeing the Mets play in 1986
was going to see a bunch of thugs
beat, brawl and humiliate their opponent

A George Foster grand-slam
followed by quiet saint Ray Knight
getting drilled by and then charging
the mound of Dodger Tom Niedenfuer

a bench-clearing, fist-flying, Shea-swinging night

Thus, spawned their bad reputation,
out there on a cool night at Shea in late May, '86

as a fan, you felt it in your bones,
a group of dangerously talented men;

There were so many heroes, games rarely mentioned
Do you remember Mookie Wilson…
-no not the slow roller-
the five hits he got in a game against the Padres?

How about Strawberry and his twenty-seven home runs
that arched over the right field wall and into the night?

And equally joyous his curtain calls,
from the dugout's top step, gracious smile,
arm raised, saluting a raucous 50,000 at Shea

The Phillies, Cubs and Cardinals
despised the ovations
but the home-runs kept coming
and with it, the curtain calls

The season was a great machine
and everyone knew their part;
the players, the fans, instinctively assumed
their role in a season that destiny had carved
for the big, bad fearsome New York Mets

Ah, yes, I remember it well!

There were games that cemented the '86 season
but remain unsung by history,
pivotal moments, turning points,
such as when Tim Teufel…

no, not the "Teufel Shuffle"
I mean the walk-off grand slam
to beat the Phillies in the bottom of the ninth!

Ah, yes, I remember it well!

And maybe the most hilarious game
of the regular season, late July
Cincinnati, the would-be last out, an error,
Mets tie game, Knight, Mitchell ejected
for fighting, Davey Johnson using pitchers
McDowell and Orosco in the outfield,
Mets score three in the fourteenth!

Ah yes, I remember it well!

And perhaps the most legendary game of
the regular season; the NL East Clincher
on September 17 at Shea Stadium
where the fans got their turn to take the field
and express the joy, the dream, the glory
of being a Mets fan, where all season long we
watched a team dominate the league,
now it was our turn to dominate the field

We wanted to reach out and touch the face of Victory
because it was as much the fans' victory
as it was the Mets' victory,
and to Doubleday and Wilpon,
we are sorry for tearing your lawn apart
we just wanted to touch, taste and smell the victory,
take it home and plant it in our yards, let it spread

into our own private Shea at home, please forgive us

The rest of the season is well documented,
worthy of another poem
which I'm sure you'll find in this book

So, again I ask, do you remeber '86?
I mean, do you *really* remember?

Letter to Family and Friends, 10/31/06

Dear Family and Friends,

Well, I have finally awoke from my Mets-loss hangover. After witnessing fifty-two games at Shea Stadium this year, another fifteen on the road and countless others on TV at home, in dingy bars and hotel rooms across the country, the season is over. At least for the Mets. Now I must endure a World Series that includes the two teams with the worst playoff record in history. Ah, the agony.

When you're a fan, there's nothing anyone could say to remedy the pain of losing such a nail-biting seventh game like the Mets did last Thursday. Truth is, there is plenty to be learned from failure. As a Mets fan, I am used to suffering epic defeats at the hands of the Yankees, Atlanta Braves and the St. Louis Cardinals. It's for that reason, the memories of triumph reign foremost in my mind. It's human nature to forget the failures and instead concentrate on our achievements. But, as my father said, "You never really experience **life** until you experience **pain.**" How true that is.

So it was at game six, with the Mets trailing the series 3-2, that I took my Mom, brothers John and Robert, sister Tammy and nephew Salvatore to Shea for a family outing of exciting October baseball. But, it wasn't just any day. It was what would be my late father's seventieth birthday. So, with the crisp autumn air and boisterous cheers of 57,000 crazed fans, it was "play-ball" for the Messina family at Shea. For me, it was a "perfect game." My family at the ballpark, my mom smiling, the Mets winning, my father looking down from the heavens, nudging me on the shoulder, "nice job, kid." I realized it couldn't get any better than that. For me, that was the defining moment of a winning season, no matter what would happen the next night.

So, when the Mets lost the following evening, yes, I was disappointed, saddened, downtrodden and feeling like I had just been sacked by the flu. I slept till noon on Friday. Finally, when I got around to checking my phone messages, nothing. It was as if everyone was thinking, "better stay away from Frank for a few days." The mailman didn't show up, the Jehovah Witnesses skipped my building. Even the garbage men stayed away, leaving my pails filled to the brim with October debris. There was an eerie, disturbing quietude in the city. One exception; the drizzle and moan of the autumn winds on Grand Street.

Turning on my computer, I avoided the news. Checking my email, one message with the header, "Mets Lament," from my buddy Mark Reese, son of Brooklyn Dodger Pee Wee Reese. A huge Dodger fan and former employee for the St. Louis Cardinals during their early 1980s heyday as the number-one Mets rival in baseball. A clever poem with the footnote, *"sorry Frank, I couldn't resist."*

Ah, the agony. Now the emails and letters come in from people I don't even know. Disgruntled Boston Red Sox fans, groveling Yank fans, someone from Virginia who writes, "Death to Mets Poetry, hahaha!" on yellow notebook paper.

But, I have crawled out from my shell and hold my head high. I openly stood up for my team, privately and public, did a great show for SNY-TV with David Amram, met Mookie Wilson, Keith Hernandez, radio hosts Steve Somers and Joe Beningo, who read my poem, "Mets Fan," on the air to millions of listeners during the Mets rally in downtown Manhattan. And even though I didn't get a chance to throw out the ceremonial first pitch at Shea, I did get the chance to bring smiles to my brothers, sister, Mom and nephew during game six. For that, I am truly grateful. Thanks to the Mets. Thanks to baseball. Thanks to everyone. The great reward of being a fan.

Love,
Frankie
10/23/06

Part IX
Full Count

Back Home in America

I had completed my mission:
seven gigs in seven nights
readings, book signings, but it
wasn't the work that tore me apart
as much as the politics, the talk;
everyone wanted to talk about
what happened to my country, my city,
my family and friends the month prior,
What happened to America?

But, it was time to come home,
attaché case filled with dog-eared texts,
love letters, maps and poems,
The plane ascends and I transcend,
pillowed against the window
under cold October morning
over black, blue Atlantic Ocean

I awake to the stinging glare of
sun shining in my eyes,
the hum of jet engines in my head
as the plane begins its initial descent,
turning south over Cape Cod,
whose curled tip unravels
into a giant sea horse, tail coursing
its way out toward the ocean

The plane dips another mile,
homes and farms become visible,

vehicles traverse the highways
of the automotive circular system,
tangling through the Adirondacks
over the great American expanse

If it weren't for all those baseball fields
checkered across the land
I may've thought I was still in Europe
-but, ah those ball fields-
no matter where you're flying over America
you'll always be able to see them,
tucked between school yards, grocery shops
city blocks and prisons,
little league, junior-high, college fields
with each passing cloud the jet flies through
another diamond, another field where dreams are born,
like the one back in Norwood
where Dad taught me how to step to the plate
and take a swing, where my brothers
were always stronger and faster,
where D and I hugged behind the dugout,
the brim of my cap bumping her forehead
with each clumsy kiss I delivered to her
rosy face under the small-town sun

The plane descends further,
New York City comes into view,
more ball fields, more dreams,
Long Island, West Islip, Flushing,
then, my childhood chapel;
dream of all dreams, Shea Stadium!
where I saw Tom Seaver

pitch a one-hitter against the Cubs in '77,
where Mom and Dad cracked peanuts open
while I tore through a giant pretzel,
the pellets shaken loose over my lap
into a miniature hailstorm

Where D and I watched the sun set
to the backdrop of Manhattan skyline,
where Joey and I skipped the fence
waited for Carter, Johnson and Strawberry,
signed our dirty one-dollar bills, ticket stubs
where Jamey, Chris, Adel and I saw the Mets clinch
the NL East in '86, thrust onto field
in a sea of fifty-thousand mad orange and blue
confetti, laughter, hugs, mayhem, Jamey disappearing
into the night, cart-wheeling across the outfield
like a circus clown; a carnival madman in the night

Yes, a place where dreams are made,
where I leaned over to brother John and shouted,
"Look, a parachutist!" as the unexpected guest
descended into the magical, rip-roar of Crazy Game Six,
where our dreams were put to the test
where John leaned to me, repeated Tug McGraw's
"You Gotta Believe!"
where I closed my eyes and said, "Do it for Bob!"
my friend, who died in a car wreck three weeks prior,
where my family stood and cheered the Mets
for all those years, cheering and believing
where years later through perseverance, turmoil
treated my own family to season tickets
where Mom, Tammy, Rob, John, Sal and I celebrated

victory
-would've been dad's seventieth birthday had he lived-
but he lived on that night, his spirit shined bright,
brother Rob, waving from the Loge across
the field from where Mom and I sat, stood, cheered
the words, "We Know" painted on the banner
where it couldn't get any better
because

-love always wins, love always wins-

in that place where dreams are made,
cultivated, celebrated, rewarded with triumph
and
now flying back home
over fields, dreams, and more fields
Yes, I had been gone too long,
my city still smoldering, still wounded
still burning, still yearning, still singing her song
as the plane lands JFK, arrival, gate, baggage,
customs, "Welcome to the United States of America"
taxicab,
radio turned on
World Series,
game seven
first pitch
back home in America
back home
in Amer-
ica

Citi Field Haiku

Thousands cross brick path
hearts beat with joy, pride, honor
a new child born

Sometimes the Diamond

Sometimes the diamond speaks to me
in the voice of an old friend,
other times in long, drawn out phrases,
foreign languages, ambiguity

Sometimes the diamond speaks to me
with the grace of art and pure mathematics,
her shadows bending toward the mound
in slow farewells to the sun

Sometimes the diamond speaks to me
in pointed, broken lines,
her symmetrical form surrendering
to the game's token rhymes

Sometimes the diamond speaks to me
in a conundrum of imperfect patience,
no matter the signals, no matter the lines
the diamond never leaves me asking, "why?"

Linda and her Father

Linda and her father never saw eye-to-eye
father's now old, ninety-two and dying

she visits father, sits by his side
"Father, you've lived such a long life"

All the years you've endured,
Great Depression, famine, World War

All the years you've enjoyed,
success, children, grandchildren

What truly stands out in your mind
as one of the special moments in your life?

the old man turns to her, looks her in the eyes,

"Going to see the Mets play at Shea Stadium, that's
what I enjoyed."

Under the Cosmic Bergen Sky

Going over the George Washington Bridge with you
is going to see God under the sheets of Spring;
no loins, no limbs, no more French kissing
just ballgame, late-night supper
and a stroll under the cosmic Bergen sky

Going over the George Washington Bridge with you
is watching the city decay under the sheets of September;
no towers, no fire escapes, no gentle affection
just ballgame, a good seventh inning stretch
and a shared smoke under the cosmic Bergen Sky

Going over the George Washington Bridge with you
is reliving a hundred nightmares, joys and sorrows;
no regrets, no lies, no quarreling with the windows down
just ballgame, a caught foul ball
and one strong hug under the cosmic Bergen sky

Going over the George Washington Bridge with you
is as glorious as it is terrible,
no failure, no triumph
just ballgame, program and scorecard
and a couple of sad laughs under the cosmic Bergen sky

The Power of Love Over Game

I got off the number seven train,
arched around the ramp,
but I couldn't get her off my mind
so I turned around, went back

Pastrami on Rye With David Amram

David and I pulled in front of the Cornelia Street Café
finishing off the last of our pastrami on rye sand-
wiches before heading into the show. We were to be
filmed for SNY-TV's Mets Weekly in a tribute to the
Mets. David was featured on piano along with his
quartet including John DeWitt on bass, Kevin Twigg
on drums and David's very own son, Adam Amram
on percussion. I was scheduled to read my new Mets
poems along with the quartet. David had his signa-
ture gig-bag of tricks, complete with penny whistles,
a dumbek, tambourine, shanai, Moroccan clay flute,
Lakota courting flute, French horn, maracas and
assorted bells and shakers.

The dashboard of his aging Subaru was layered with
his new piano concerto, manuscripts, sheet music, cof-
fee napkins and discarded wrappers from Mamoun's
Falafel. An empty bottle of Dr. Brown's Black Cherry
Soda clanged back and forth
under the seat as David maneuvered the car into the
parking spot that was miraculously and suddenly
made available in pure David-Amram-New-York-City-
spontaneous-fashion. Anyone else would've had to circle
around the block for a year before finding a spot. How-
ever, Saint David always finds one as if ghost-angels
themselves personally part the Red Sea of Cornelia
Street for him.

A packed house awaited us, but I managed to bounce
one question off David before heading in. I asked what
his dear friend, the writer Jack Kerouac, might have

thought about modern baseball, particularly the salaries of baseball players.

"I think Jack would say the same thing that Pee Wee Reese would say when he was asked a similar question in the documentary film, Boys of Winter, produced by Pee Wee's son, Mark Reese. To paraphrase Pee Wee, 'I love the game, and I always will. If these young men are helping to fill up the stadium and getting their fair share, all I say is go get 'em boys'."

David sinks teeth into sandwich.

"I could never speak for another person
but I'm quite certain Jack Kerouac would be happy
to see athletes getting the attention and respect they deserve. Jack was a hometown football hero and knew how fleeting that can be. He took that same energy and dedication and used it in his work. The same sense of sportsmanship that has almost disappeared from our vocabulary, he saw it as an extension of human loving kindness."

Another bite of the sandwich.

"As for the future of the game, he saw the same thing in general society. Because greed and narcissism had already been there. Shakespeare and Dostoyevsky spoke about this. The un-sportsmanlike swine as apposed to the sportsman lover of the game, lover of young people who expect the art and fellowship of the game. Just as a fellowship among all artists and writers, Jack was a true sportsman."

"The real artists, the real athletes, the ones that work hard and show up every day to perform instead of griping and complaining, the ones that are there at the end of the ninth with the bases loaded, they're the ones that can drive in the winning run. For those young men and women today, it's great to see them paid their just amount."

One last bite and a crumple of a napkin.

"In all the sleaze that's gone into that bulging landfill that we sometimes mistake for cultural history, along with all the other pollution we've created, the sun will still be shining, baseball will still be a great inspiration as it was to Jack and I in our boyhood and will always remain a beautiful game. For those that complain that the game is too slow, they have to get themselves together, calm down and pay attention. Beethoven and Shakespeare are not too slow, they're right on time. And as Charlie Parker said in 1945, 'now's the time'."

I gulped down the last bite of pastrami on rye, opened the car door, helped David carry his array of musical instruments through the building, down the narrow staircase and into the warm, friendly embrace of Cornelia Street Café .

A producer from SNY stopped David, asked him what he thinks about baseball. I knew there was time for at least one beer before show time to wash down the pastrami on rye. I pulled up a chair, kicked back and let the rhythm of the evening discover its own mystery.

And a Dream That Lasts

I am blue black Mets cap
on the hook, off the chart,
in gym bag, abandoned, lost-and-found,
again and again, I wander and wait,
wander until the sun rises, sets
and I become one with the game,
the dust of the departed ones

She came out to speak, sing, softly
D in the midnight, with ball and glove
and a dream of singing in the rain
and steel gray, tasting drops
in corners of mouth, cloud cover
rainbow, sun setting, love abound

Threaded needle, beckon my return
but I cannot return to where dreams
were built, the house they took it down,
The scoreboard fell in clouded storm,
no hiking through the jungled past
only tomorrow and a dream that lasts!

Refreshed, We Come

We the people, 2009
new year, new president,
new season, new ballpark,
refreshed, we come
through melting snow,
the birds of spring perched
with open wings
on Opening Day at Citi Field

We the people, 2009
our team, our time
rise up, walk forward
and greet the new day
with open arms, embrace
this moment
of hope and grace
on Opening Day at Citi Field

We the people, 2009
celebrate, congregate, for this sanctuary
shall be our home, our church
of America's pastime, a tree
whose roots run deep in history
and even deeper in the hearts of
every child who dreams the impossible
on Opening Day at Citi Field

We the people, 2009
welcome our families, friends,
our leaders, our heroes
those who serve and in memory

of those who died,
new season, new year, new ballpark
refreshed, we come
through melting snow
on Opening Day at Citi Field

We the people, refreshed, we come
uphold the spirit of our city,
devotion to our beloved team
we ask God's blessing
on this magical, spring day
we, the people, refreshed we come
through melting snow
on Opening Day at Citi Field

Love Always Wins

D and I shuffled
through the Gate B turnstile,
passed scorecard barkers,
up the Field Level ramp
until the ball field
blossomed before our eyes
like a big, happy sunflower

D bought "dogs" and I splurged for the beers
then weaved our way to our seats
through a fabric of orange and blue

We high-fived and cheered
shared laughs, days of old
our team didn't win that night,
but our hearts overflowed with the joy
of being together like ageless
children under the stars

After the game
-to Arturo's for pizza and jazz-
the band kicked into
a bebop tempo, made us jiggle
and swing between bites of tangy slices
and sips of sweet sangria

The band rocked and swayed
-piano legend himself Harry Whitaker-
leaned into keys like a wild man
hanging his jawed-out jowls

closer and closer to the keys,
eyebrows rising and falling
with each chord banged out of the body
of the black baby grand
angelic expressions,
ecstatic, out-of-body expressions
that formed into a halo of musical notes
over his head, held in place by the hand of God

The bass player walked his fingers
up and down the instrument
intonating Es, Bs and even high Cs

Contorting face, right leg hugging bass
as the drummer high-hatted, snared his way
shoulders rocking from sockets like a mad machine;
a steam engine, the wheels of a locomotive,
he tipped and tapped, eyes closed
in a state of holy roller convulsive,
Bodhisattva-like nirvana

D and I shook more shoulders
slipped another slice, hot pepper, oregano,
grated parmesan, fresh basil, smoky coal oven crust
Tony shot us a round on the house
Gina spun a serving tray on one finger
balancing, spinning like a flying saucer
while Angel snaked between musicians, patrons
exchanging "how-do-you-do's" in one motion
while Scotty (Alligator-Eyes), back pressed to jukebox
arms crossed like a prison guard, sported a mug with
one eye on the band, the other on the cash register

"keep it ringing, keep it ringing!"
and
Jimmy Latigano, who cries when he smiles
and smiles when he sings "Stormy Weather"
like a Harlequin, a cabaret showman
-song fueled by joy and sorrow-
the utter guttural moan of melancholy
nailing the last verse and
as the sky bursts open

 "It's pouring out!" smiled D
the drops came down in long silver threads
pounding the pavement in one continuous clatter
while girls in summer dresses and boys in fancied jeans
crouched for cover under Arturo's friendly, red awning

In one last dance, we paid our tab,
kissed, waved, then swished from puddled curb
straight through a sheet of blasted rain
that shattered the beams of headlights
into a dizzy of diamonds on Houston Street

We walked for blocks like mad children
who'd just been let out of school, the doors of our lives
swung wide off their hinges, clothes soaked to our skin

A young chap and his gal huddled
in the alcove of a chic bar entrance
on West Broadway slipped a phrase that resonated
through the raindrops like a harmonic off a guitar
"You cats got the right idea," he said
Then flicked his cigarette to the street,

its cinder doused before it hit the ground

D and I left the chap and his gal
huddled in the chic bar entrance,
and laughed into the night like mad fools
-mad fools in the rain-
free of the pain of loss,
and the desire to win,
and all those miserable things
that drive people insane
No, we had already won,
the night was ours
and we set it on fire
with the beauty of our love

About the Author

Frank Messina, "The Mets Poet," has appeared on SNY-TV, the station that broadcasts Mets games, in video montages that feature him reciting his poetry against the visual backdrop of glorious moments in Mets baseball. An award-winning poet and performer, he travels worldwide giving poetry readings (not all of his work deals with the Mets) and readily admits that much of his Mets poetry is driven by the passion of being a diehard fan of a team that repeatedly endures dramatic victory and defeat like no other sports team.